AS A TREE GROWS

As a Tree Grows

Reflections on Growing in the
Image of Christ

W. Phillip Keller

This special Billy Graham Evangelistic Association
edition is published with permission from the author
W. Phillip Keller.

CONTENTS

Foreword

DEEP WITHIN THE INNERMOST HEART of every earnest child of God there lies a compelling urge, an aroused desire, to become more like Christ in character.

The pages that follow show in simple layman's language how one can grow in godliness. By comparing parallel principles of natural growth in the life of a tree with supernatural truth in the life of a believer the manner in which a Christian character develops is made clear.

This method of demonstrating divine truth through natural phenomena was frequently used by Christ himself when he walked among men. Being the author of both the natural and supernatural realms it was the most effective means of conveying His truth to human hearts.

May these woodsman's insights into how the child of God can "grow like a cedar in Lebanon" assist the reader to become more like the Master.

W. PHILLIP KELLER

7

The Cedars of Lebanon

The righteous shall flourish like the palm tree: he shall grow like a cedar in Lebanon—Ps 92:12

WHAT A CLEAR, CONCISE STATEMENT! "The righteous [the man or woman right with God; a person in whom has been implanted a new, spiritual life by God's Spirit] *shall grow* like a cedar in Lebanon."

The cedars of Lebanon are referred to frequently in Scripture. They are unique trees of breathtaking beauty, massive size, rich fragrance, and high-quality timber. Their natural habitat is the high mountainous country of Lebanon where they grow luxuriantly.

The cedars of Lebanon are used as a symbol of all that is to be desired in Christian character. They stand for that which is fine and noble and strong. They represent beauty of life, vigor of character, fragrance of personality, and impeccability of conduct.

If I am utterly honest with my own heart I shall discover that my character as a Christian is not of this caliber. I lack the qualities which would ordinarily make me stand out above my fellows as the cedars stand tall above the lesser trees and vegetation growing about their base.

This need not be so. We have the authority of God's declaration that it is normal for anyone who has *new* life from above, implanted within the soul by the Spirit of God, to grow into a mature Christlike individual. "The righteous shall grow . . . like a cedar in Lebanon."

A tiny cedar seedling, by growing steadily and surely, matures into a mighty monarch of the mountain forest. But the tragedy is that some never get much beyond being tiny, stunted seedlings. They are alive; they are true trees; but they are virtually standing still. There is no growth.

For the cedars to become impressive trees, inspiring in their stature, strong in their timber, they must grow far beyond seedling or even sapling stage. They simply have to put on annual growth rings to produce towering trunks from which fine lumber can be cut. And this they do naturally and quietly without fanfare or frustration. It is a normal process. Similarly there should be a natural growth in the Christian's character.

In the Old Testament the details of the construction of Solomon's temple in Jerusalem are carefully recorded. We are told that the outer walls were of stone, a product of the earth, earthy. All of the stonework on the inside of the temple was to be covered with cedar boards and beams. This timber was obtained from the magnificent cedars of Lebanon. King Solomon went to great expense and labor to have these trees cut and transported from the mountains of Lebanon down to Jerusalem because there was no substitute for this wood.

Then, finally, the cedar lining of the walls was in turn overlaid with pure gold. Thus the temple became a suitable sanctuary for the Most High God.

This is a precise picture of the normal Christian. My physical body is of the earth, earthy. "For dust thou art, and unto dust shalt thou return" (Ge 3:19). This is the counterpart of the temple's outer walls of stone.

As an infant I entered the world with an earthborn frame of flesh within which resides an undeveloped character bearing a most remarkable capacity for God and for growth.

The cedar boards and beams were produced from living trees that had grown in the high mountains. So, likewise, through the growth of godly character it is intended that I should become a fit habitation for God himself. To be suited for this noble service my life must possess qualities comparable to those of the cedars of Lebanon.

What are these special characteristics, and why was it imperative that cedar be used in the temple?

First of all, this timber is rich-grained, lustrous, and beautiful to behold. Is this true of my character? Is there a glow, an attractiveness, to my life?

Second, cedar has a delicate aroma, a delightful fragrance. This perfume permeated the whole building. Are those around me conscious of the fragrance of Christ in my character?

Third, the cedar is famous for its repulsion of insects of all sorts. Moths and beetles and termites avoid it. Its presence has a purifying influence. Does mine, in a sordid, corrupt world?

Fourth, the cedar of Lebanon is a very durable wood, being quite impervious to decay. If my character is Christlike it will have this enduring quality. It will not be weak or soft or rotten.

Inside Solomon's splendid temple the cedar boards were in turn overlaid with pure gold. In

God's language gold represents purity, holiness, righteousness—the righteousness of God himself. There is applied to my character the righteousness of Christ Jesus—the overlaying of my life with the holiness of himself. Thus I become a fit habitation for God. "Ye are the temple of the living God; as God hath said, I will dwell in them, and walk in them" (2 Cor 6:16).

This, then, being the parallel, how do the cedars of Lebanon grow into maturity for such a noble purpose? If they, through patient growth, produced fine material for the temple, then I, too, through growth must be capable of developing a character for holy service.

A tree grows, as does a soul, not by internal striving, but by continuous response to certain external stimuli outside itself. In the natural as in the supernatural (spiritual) realm there are specific conditions which must be present to insure optimum growth. These will now be examined individually as they apply to the character of a Christian.

Life

God gave us eternal life, and this life is in His Son. He who possesses the Son has that life; he who does not possess the Son of God does not have that life—1 Jn 5:11-12, Amplified Bible

AN OBVIOUS TRUTH, though one that is sometimes forgotten, is the fact that growth is impossible without *LIFE* being present. Only a live organism is able to grow. Therefore, it follows that the first requirement for growth is *life*.

The life of a cedar commences in the cone of a

parent tree. Within the tiny seed, packed tightly inside the cone of the mature tree, lies the minute life-germ implanted there through the complex and mysterious reproductive process of heredity.

When the cone has ripened and fully matured it opens under the impulse of sunshine, moisture, and moving air. The small seed is released to the wind and floats down to earth where it will find its seedbed upon the forest floor. Lying there so very small and insignificant it holds within itself *life*; it possesses a potential cedar tree within its very germ. Yet to the untrained eye of the casual passerby it may appear inert and unpromising.

All that is required, however, is for the appropriate natural environment to exert its influence on the life within the seed and it will begin to be a tree. As the germ responds to the stimuli of moisture, warmth, air, and light which surround it, germination takes place and growth commences.

This is how a tree begins.

This is how the life of a tree develops.

But, what is life?

We really do not know! Immense sums of money and millions of man-hours of research have been spent attempting to discover what *life* really is. We know what it does and how it responds to various stimuli, and on this basis we have produced a fairly simple scientific definition for it:

Life is the capacity of an organism to correspond with its environment.

So when the tiny, viable seed finds itself surrounded by an array of stimuli such as moisture, air, warmth, light, and others which comprise its total environment, it responds. It germinates. It begins to grow. One day a slender rootlet emerges and starts to grow down into the soil. Soon after, a frail shoot pushes out and upward reaching toward the sun. A seedling is under way! If all goes well its root will penetrate the forest floor while at the same time its first frail leaves will spread themselves in the air. Slowly, surely, and with quiet persistence it grows first into a seedling, then a sapling, then a sturdy tree, and at last a forest monarch.

All this growth, all this maturity, is the outcome of correspondence between the tree and its environment.

In truth it may be said that not only does the tree penetrate directly into its environment but also that, as we shall see in later chapters, the components of the environment actually enter intimately into the tree thus producing normal growth. This is correspondence between the two.

Now, just as the parent cedar produces certain cones carrying viable seeds that have implanted in them the life germ of a new cedar, so God the Father, by his Holy Spirit, implants in the hearts of some men—those who believe—the very life of

Christ, the *LIFE* of God himself from above. How?

"It is the spirit which gives Life; the flesh confers no benefit whatever. The words I have spoken to you are spirit and Life. But there are some of you who do not believe." (Jn 6:63-64, Weymouth N.T.)

This "inheritance" of eternal life is a mystery and marvel that even surpasses the hereditary process within the seed of a cedar. No more does the frail, minute, inert-looking seed lying on the ground resemble the magnificent tree towering above it than does a newborn Christian (believer in Christ) resemble the mighty God, the Heavenly Father, whose will it is that he, likewise, should develop into his likeness. It is not the outer appearance which matters. It is, rather, the imparting of God's own life to mortal man, enabling him to have correspondence with God, that counts.

The vital question is, Do I have this *LIFE*?

The verse at the head of this study puts it very plainly.

"He who does not possess the Son of God does not have that life."

Beneath the giant, outstretched limbs of the parent cedar there may be thousands of seeds scattered upon the earth. Yet out of these only a few dozen may be viable (possessing life). All were produced by the tree, but not all will become new trees. Some lack *life*.

The same is true of people. God makes it very clear that, though he is the Father of all men by creation, only those to whom *the life of Christ* has been vitally imparted are spiritually alive. All others are dead. This sobering truth confronts every individual.

We stand in amazement before the realization that God the Father purposes, desires, and wills that we should develop our inherent capacity to become like himself. Yet this is only possible if first we have his life in us. He yearns to give us the *GIFT OF LIFE.* Nothing thrills him more than to see us accept Christ who becomes our *NEW LIFE.* This remains one of the moving mysteries of human history (see Eph 1). The realization that the all-wise, all-loving, all-righteous, all-powerful One should choose to impart to man not only his own divine life but also the capacity to mature into his own likeness overwhelms the human heart.

This new, inner life is in reality the very Spirit of Christ himself imparted to mortal man. This is what is meant by "receiving Christ" into the heart. It is achieved through the invasion of man's spirit by the Spirit of the living God. Only the Spirit of God occupying and controlling the spirit of a man makes that man capable of responding to the stimuli which, surrounding him on every side, emanate from God. This correspondence with God is the normal Christian life. It is what Scripture calls walking with God or "fellowship . . . with the Father" or being "alive unto God."

A genuine Christian moves and lives and has his being in God (Acts 17:28). God becomes his very environment. And it is only in this atmosphere that he grows in Christ.

Water

Blessed is the man that trusteth in the Lord, and whose hope the Lord is. For he shall be as a tree planted by the waters, and that spreadeth out her roots by the river, and shall not see when heat cometh, but her leaf shall be green; and shall not be careful in the year of drought, neither shall cease from yielding fruit.

—Jer 17:7-8

THE VITAL LIFE PROCESSES of an organism are dependent on moisture in its cells. Water is essential to survival. A flourishing tree may be 80 percent moisture, which means that there must be a continuous supply available from its environment if growth is to proceed normally.

Water spells the difference between a desert and a forest. It spells the difference between a dry, shriveled, stunted tree and the splendid form of a towering cedar of Lebanon. Water is actually the essence of life within a growing tree.

Not only is moisture essential as that which combines with the air to produce carbohydrates for growth, but it is also the means of food and energy exchange within the tree. In addition, it guarantees mineral and vitamin absorption through both the leaves and roots. It determines the health and vigor of the tree.

A healthy tree has its cells turgid and charged with moisture. The sap which circulates throughout the tree is a complex combination of minerals, carbohydrates, vitamins, and proteins in suspension. The constant movement of this moisture through the tree from cell to cell conditions and controls its health.

All trees, like the cedars of Lebanon, may derive water from their environment in a variety of ways. The water may be in the form of the still, silvery dew that descends during the night to settle softly on the outstretched boughs. It may be in the clouds and mists and fog that sweep in off the sea to swathe the forest in misty veils. It may be the summer showers or the winter snows. It may come through underground springs or rushing streams that cascade down the mountainside, where roots reach out to draw refreshment from the flow.

But a point to remember is that the tree does not hoard this moisture for itself. The vast network of running roots beneath the soil often exceeds the outspread canopy of trunk, branches, and leaves spread to the sky. And vast quantities of water are lifted through the framework of the tree to be transpired out into the surrounding air. This moisture, along with the discharge of oxygen, is what gives the forest atmosphere such a fresh fragrance.

Again we discover striking parallels in the life of the eager, earnest Christian who is thirsting after righteousness, eager to grow into the likeness of Christ.

God's Word tells us explicitly that such shall be satisfied. "Blessed are they which do hunger and thirst after righteousness: for they shall be filled" (Mt 5:6).

Again, in Isaiah 44:3, "For I will pour water upon him that is thirsty, and floods upon the dry ground."

In the spiritual realm, what is the counterpart of water to a tree?

It is life eternal. It is everlasting life. It is the very resurrection life of Christ himself imparted to mortal man. It is new life in Christ made available to me by his death and through his blood shed on Calvary.

Throughout Scripture we have the picture given to us of Christ himself being the true fountain of living water (Jer 2:13). He is shown as the source and spring of everlasting life which is poured out continuously to thirsty men and women (Rev 22:1). Without this invigorating flow of life I am spiritually desiccated (dried up). I live amid a world in which the mark of death and decay lies upon everything that surrounds me. I am like a tree in a desert spot languishing for water.

But Christ deigned to come down into this earthly domain of death. He chose to deliberately pour out his life in his blood in order to deliver me from death. Now, through his resurrection power, his life eternal flows forever to those who will draw on it.

As a tree by the waters grows, in spite of drought all around it, so I, by drawing upon the life of Christ, grow into his strength and beauty despite the dominion of death all around me.

How do I do this in a practical way?

In Scripture, *to drink is to believe.*

First, I believe that by Christ's shed blood the *penalty* of death which would otherwise be mine for past sins has been canceled at Calvary.

Second, I claim a daily energizing through the

resurrection life of Christ made real in me by his Spirit. This keeps me from the *power* of sin and evil, which would otherwise stunt my Christian life.

The moisture which a tree took in last week will not suffice for today. Likewise, I, too, must draw daily on the water of divine life—even on Christ's refreshing stream.

This process of receiving continuously the very life of Christ is to be made keenly aware of his presence and power within. I have the work of Calvary cleansing me from the *guilt* of sins, and I have the resurrection life of Christ (made real in me by the Spirit) ever keeping me from the *grip* of sin. Thus I live a triumphant life of true health and holiness in God. This is how I rise above the world.

Just as water is lifted high in the tallest cedar against all the downward pull of gravity, so the triumphant life of Christ is uplifted in me through the upwelling life of his Spirit within. He it is who counteracts all the downward drag of sin and death in the decadent world around me (see Romans 8:2).

To live thus, cleansed and enlivened by the water of life which flows continually from Christ for thirsty men, is to live and grow up in him. What is more, it is to have springing up from within my innermost being a surge of life that flows out (is transpired) to those around me in refreshment and benediction.

"The man who believes in me, as the scripture said, will have rivers of living water flowing from his inmost heart" (Jn 7:38, Phillips translation).

Light

All things were made by him; and without him was not anything made that was made.

In him was life; and the life was the light of men.

And the light shineth in darkness; and the darkness comprehended it not—Jn 1:3-5

IN THE PHYSICAL REALM of plants, shrubs, and trees, light is the key to life. Without light there can be only degeneration and death.

If we study the association of trees and shrubs

in a forest we will soon discover that each one is competing with its fellows for light. *Each* is stretching out its limbs and leaves to capture the maximum amount of available sunlight.

The lower limbs and smaller trees growing in the understory of the forest where there is only feeble light filtering through the overhanging foliage will be stunted and sickly and susceptible to disease.

On the upper surface of each leaf or needle are an innumerable array of stomata with light-absorbing cells. By means of the complex process of photosynthesis sunlight is used by the leaf to produce carbohydrates for its growth.

This explains why, in order to flourish and grow, a leaf automatically responds to light falling upon it and turns toward it.

Almost all of us have seen plants in a window turn all their leaves toward the sun. A leaf that does not respond to this outer stimulus is sick.

Likewise most of us have seen plants that were kept in a basement or darkened room where there was insufficient light. They were yellow and sickly and made no strong growth.

It is worthy of mention here that the basis of all plant and animal life upon our planet is inexorably locked up with light. Light is the catalyst which accounts ultimately for the production of organic growth in all its diverse forms. It is this response to light that stimulates and accelerates growth. It enables a seedling to grow from a tiny green spike, pushing its way up through the damp mold of the forest floor, to a majestic monarch of a tree that combs the clouds with its upstretched limbs.

The majestic cedars of Lebanon, their great, widespread limbs reaching into the sunny skies of northern Palestine, are in reality stretching toward the sun. Every live twig and needle they possess turns to the precise position where it will benefit most from the sunlight streaming down upon it.

Response to sunlight year after year is part of the secret of their stature.

In the realm of the supernatural (spiritual) life the same identical principle of growth holds true. We are told emphatically in the verses at the head of this chapter that God is life and this life was the light of men.

Elsewhere the Word of God states plainly:

"The Lord God is a sun . . . " (Ps 84:11).

He is the source of all life, both physical and spiritual. He surrounds us on every side with the radiance of himself.

Spiritual light, divine light, God-given light, can reach our hearts in a number of ways.

First and foremost there is the earthly life, ministry, death, resurrection, and message of Jesus Christ. He was the literal expression of divine life and light in human form.

Second, there is the written Word of God in Scripture, which again is referred to as light.

Then there is the spoken message and live reality of godly preachers, teachers, and Christian friends conveying light to our hearts.

Finally there is the realm of nature, which reveals the unity, beauty, and wisdom of the character of God himself.

Through all these media light is continually being shed about me. Now the important and crucial question is: Do I respond to the light that falls upon my heart and mind? Do I turn toward it? Do I reach out for it and hold myself in readiness to react to its stimulus?

How does one respond to spiritual light so that its entrance will produce growth of character?

Here is a simple illustration. Suppose my character is continually marred by my caustic tongue. Not only can it carve up my acquaintances but it continually brings reproach on my Master.

Then one day the light of God's Word on this matter suddenly streams into my aroused consciousness from James 3.

I am faced with two choices. Either I can turn away from this light, spurn it, ignore it, excuse myself by saying, "Oh, well, that's just a weakness of mine." Or I can turn toward God on this point in repentance. I can allow the light to penetrate to the bottom of my being about this matter. I reach out in genuine repentance (an absolute, sincere decision to quit) and embrace the light. At the same time I ask that the gracious Holy Spirit empower me to control my conduct.

This is faith in action.

Faith in action is the Christian's response to light. And the moment I respond thus, God gives power (for light is energy) to grow on this point.

To merely feel sorry for having offended someone with my tongue and then to return and do the same again is neither to repent, nor to respond to light, nor to grow in this area of my life.

It is in fact to fold up and wilt just as a leaf does which refuses sunlight. This denotes that I am sick and weak.

The remarkable truth about exposure to light, whether in the natural or supernatural, is that the growth produced by it is the actual transmutation of light. The tree itself is transformed into a light-storing, light-giving body. This is shown when we burn a slab of wood and see its flames give off light energy accumulated through many summers of patient growth.

Likewise, my character is changed and transformed into the very character of God when continually exposed to him. Paul stated this clearly when he said, "And all of us, with unveiled faces, reflecting like bright mirrors the glory [character] of the Lord, are being transformed into the same likeness, from one degree of holiness to another, even as derived from the Lord the Spirit" (2 Cor 3:18, Weymouth N.T.).

Heat

And they said one to another, Did not our heart burn within us, while he talked with us by the way, and while he opened to us the scriptures?
—Lk 24:32

THE NEXT REQUIREMENT for growth is heat. A tree may be flooded with light but unless the temperature is above 40 degrees F. there will be little or no growth.

When trees grow at very high altitudes on mountains or on the fringe of the true Arctic zones they are dwarfed and stunted by cold. A transect taken from one of these little scrawny trees may show it to be several hundred years old, yet it may be no more than six or eight feet high.

But the cedars of Lebanon have the benefit of being native to a warm and sunny climate. They enjoy a long growing season during which the weather is balmy and conducive to growth most of the year.

As in the case of light, the tree or its leaves are incapable of growth, even in the summer, unless there is a proper internal response to the warmth around them. Only a healthy tree is sensitive to the stimulus of heat.

Each stoma of a leaf has two guard cells at its entrance which open or close in response to temperature change. When they open it is possible for air to enter the leaf, allowing the process of photosynthesis to proceed. This process is said to be the most important on the planet, since all plant as well as animal life depends upon it for growth and sustenance.

A healthy, vigorous tree is sensitive to the temperature around it. It responds eagerly to warmth, allowing the full flow of air to enter its stomata, thus producing maximum growth.

Turning to the Christian life, it is a sad but true observation that there are innumerable Christians with stunted, dwarfed characters like a tree at timberline. They may have been exposed to a tremendous amount of light all their lives but there has been virtually no growth. In fact, some have literally stood still, unmoving and unchanged, from the time of their beginning a new life in Christ. They are really not more than seedlings or spindly saplings from which little timber can come to fashion a temple of the Most High.

This lack of maturity in Christian character brings contempt upon the church. Many who claim to have known the Lord for twenty, thirty, or forty years, have characters which are a mockery because there has been no growth, nor change, no transformation into the likeness of Christ.

In looking back to my youth, I am reminded again and again of the tremendous impact made on my own life by watching the growth in my father's Christian character. As a small lad I knew him to be a hard-driving, hotheaded, impulsive, impatient man. But as I grew up and passed through my teens I watched, awe-struck, at a steady transformation taking place in my father. It was obvious that the love of God was being shed abroad more and more in his life and in responding to that love, his character was changed. He became one of the most gentle, endearing, considerate, and warmhearted people I ever knew.

In the Christian life, the counterpart of physical warmth is love or affection. It is the other side of the character of God himself—"for God is love" (1 Jn 4:8).

Just as God is light, which reveals to us his character of holiness, purity, justice, and righteousness, so God is love, which discloses his character of compassion, mercy, tenderness, and kindness.

There are Christians who know all about God in a clinical way. They can dispute over doctrines and discuss all the details related to the divine life. There is no end to the light they have, but it has never produced growth because it was not combined with a warm, personal love for Christ.

Just as a tree surrounded with summer sunlight grows rapidly in response to light and warmth, so can I grow as a Christian the moment I respond to the love of God which surrounds me on every side.

The love of God to men is a continuous outpouring just as are the warm rays of sunlight from the sun. This outpouring finds expression in a myriad of forms. It is the food I eat, the heat for my home, the air I breathe, the water I drink, my friends and my family, my faculties of sight, sound, and sense. In fact, "every good and every perfect gift is from above, and cometh down from the Father of lights" (Jas 1:17).

God's love to us, however, found its most

poignant and sublime expression in his own Son who came to live among men, then die and rise again, to make it possible for us to share his eternal life.

How then do I respond to this love? How do I react so that it will produce growth in my character?

As with light so with love, I must hold myself open to allow it to enter—for love begets love.

This is done by deliberately maintaining what I call "an attitude of gratitude."

If I determine, by God's help, to discover something good from him for which to be genuinely grateful in every event and circumstance of life, it will surprise me to feel my heart warmed toward him. This will result in an inner glow of gratitude.

Instead of complaining I will find myself thanking him for his kindness and mercy and love each day.

To do this is to grow in love and affection and warmth, not only to Christ but also to those around me.

True appreciation is one certain way to give great pleasure and love back to my Heavenly Father.

What is more, in this sort of inner climate, compounded of love and appreciation, the gracious Holy Spirit comes into my being eager to produce his own fruits of a sunnier clime.

This is to know what it is to have our hearts burn within us, moved by a warm, compelling affection for Christ—growing in gratitude and graciousness.

Air

And the Lord formed man of the dust of the ground, and breathed into his nostrils the breath of life; and man became a living soul—Ge 2:7

IN THE DISCUSSION of growth in response to light it was pointed out that the critical process of photosynthesis involves the combination of carbon dioxide and water into carbohydrates under the stimulus of sunlight.

The carbon dioxide for this purpose is drawn by the plant directly from the atmosphere which surrounds it, and is absorbed by the stomata of the leaf when the guard cells open.

As the plant extracts the carbon dioxide from the air, it discharges back into the atmosphere pure oxygen. In part, this is how the oxygen content of the atmosphere is maintained. The balance of the oxygen content of the air which is so essential to all life on earth is controlled to a very large extent by the growth processes of plants and trees.

It is also this discharge of oxygen into the atmosphere which gives that special quality of purity and freshness to forest and mountain air. There is an exciting invigoration and keen stimulation to the atmosphere of forested country.

Most of us are acquainted with the perfumelike pungence of a pine or fir forest that is breathing deeply of summer air. The trees are growing at a maximum rate, drawing heavily from the warm, sunlit air that surrounds them. No matter what species the tree may be, this is the season of setting and forming and ripening its fruit.

Again, as with light or warmth, the degree of growth and its effect on the tree are related to the response of the tree to the air around it.

Scientific experiments have demonstrated that a tree absorbs much more than merely carbon dioxide from the air that moves about its limbs. Borne upon the winds, especially those from off the sea, or ocean, are minute particles of minerals in suspension of mist and fog. These are picked up from the wind-plowed surfaces of the sea to be carried aloft in clouds. Nutrients are thus combed from the atmoshere by the eager, grasping, waving branches that bow and bend beneath the whispering winds.

This is also part of the secret of the majestic growth of the giant cedars of the high country.

Throughout the Word of God the gracious Holy Spirit is likened to air, to atmosphere, to the wind. "The wind breathes where it will, and thou canst hear the sound of it, but knowest nothing of the way it came or the way it goes; so it is, when a man is born by the breath of the Spirit" (Jn 3:8, Knox translation).

To every true child of God come continually the soft solicitations of the Holy Spirit. He comes with gentleness yet with an insistent desire to be allowed admittance into the innermost recesses of the life and heart and intellect.

In the providential plan of God the choice of whether or not an individual will allow the gracious Spirit to enter is a matter of personal cooperation. As pointed out in the preceding chapter, if we are warm in our affection and love and gratitude to God we provide a welcome climate within. Here the Spirit finds it not only easy to enter, but also conducive to the production of his own exotic fruits.

"The Spirit, however, produces in human life

fruits such as these: love, joy, peace, patience, kindness, generosity, fidelity, tolerance and self-control" (Gal 5:22, Phillips translation).

If we would grow and produce these fruits, the one thing we must do is draw deeply of the Spirit of Life himself who is willing to enter the waiting heart that is open to him with a warm welcome.

How is this done in practical experience?

The areas of my spiritual life which can be made open and available to him are my mind, my intellect, my emotions, and my will.

These all have their seat in my conscious and subconscious mind. It is perfectly possible for me to deliberately respond to the wooing of the gracious Spirit as he speaks to my innermost mind. Or, conversely, I can spurn and reject his overtures. If I do the latter he is easily grieved and quickly withdraws. He will not force an entrance or impose himself upon me.

If I wish to have a Christian mind marked by the qualities of the mind of Christ, it is proper for the production of such a mind to come about by the inner working of the gracious Spirit in my mind. My appetites, my desires, my ambitions, my motives, will be molded and made up of impulses which had their origin with him. The degree to which this is done daily in my life is proportional to the degree to which I deliberately allow him to enter and control my mind, emotions, and will.

Not only will this result in my thinking upon those things which are pure and lovely and of good report but it will mean my entire life exudes a wholesome aura of decency and uplift and integrity. To be with me will be akin to walking amid the cedars of Lebanon—which are both noble and fragrant—trees of the high places. This is to know something of the secret growth in godliness.

The question is, have I ever sincerely and earnestly invited the Holy Spirit to occupy and take control of my mind in this manner? He awaits my invitation to enter and begin his own winsome work of growth. It is he who will give me a godly disposition.

"For it is God which worketh in you both to will and to do of his good pleasure" (Phil 2:13).

Weather

Praise the Lord from the earth ye dragons, and all deeps: fire, and hail; snow, and vapours; stormy wind fulfilling his word: mountains, and all hills; fruitful trees, and all cedars.

—Ps 148:7-9

WEATHER IS A MOST IMPORTANT and ever present part of any environment in which a tree grows. Up to this stage in our studies we have discussed the specific components which comprise weather as a whole: heat, light, moisture, air.

There is, however, an overall sense in which weather is a direct physical force influencing the growth of a tree. Storms, hail, blizzards, sleet, snow, frost, or lashing winds make an inescapable impact upon all plant life, but especially on trees that are long-lived. They must stand exposed to the whims of weather year after year, unable to escape or evade its onslaught, facing its fury with quiet fortitude.

Often as a boy I would lie in the shade of some sturdy tree that stood alone, green and strong beneath the blazing sun, wondering what it would be like to be a tree. I knew that for the tree there could be no release from the spot in the soil to which it was rooted. It simply had to stand there silently, enduring the burning heat and searing drought of summer. When autumn winds lashed its limbs, stripping off its tattered leaves, there was still no escape. Under the blast of winter blizzards, with their weight of snow and frost and sleet, it could only bow its branches, sometimes bent to its tired trunk, and wait patiently for release. And then again, March gales and April storms would whip it mercilessly, glazing it in ice before its buds at last began to burst anew in spring. Always, patiently, heroically, it endured all sorts of weather.

Not until later in life, when I began serious mountain climbing, did I fully understand what weather could do to wood. High up on the hills, well above the thick forest stands, where individual trees stood exposed on some rugged ridge, I found trees of exquisite beauty and matchless character. There they stood, their forms twisted and battered into striking shapes. Here was the stuff to delight an artist, the beauty to challenge a photographer.

But beside this, all the fury of sleet and wind and snow and sun had fashioned an inner beauty beyond belief.

Here was wood with grain of luster and lovely lines. Wood with whirls and curves that would delight the heart of a wood-carver—even those old craftsmen who carved the flowers and fruits that were to adorn the inner sanctuary of Solomon's temple.

Turning to the normal life of the Christian we are confronted with the simple fact that in this life we are going to have troubles. Jesus himself said, "In the world ye shall have tribulation: but be of good cheer; I have overcome the world" (Jn 16:33).

The life of our Lord himself was, outwardly, a continuous series of testings and turmoil. He was a virtual storm center about which there raged relentlessly all the fury of his enemies and detractors. Yet within there was the quiet acceptance of every adversity as a part of the Father's will.

In another place he told his followers in very straightforward language, "If the world hates you, ye know that it hated me before it hated you" (Jn 15:18).

One of the fallacious concepts that has crept into the church is that if a man becomes a Christian, then everything in life's garden will suddenly become agreeable and delightful; that there will be nothing but blessing and prosperity and peacefulness.

This is simply not so, and more especially for the man or woman courageous enough to take an open stand, set apart from the crowd, where the blasts of criticism, scorn, and ridicule of a cynical world will be felt at their fiercest.

But exactly as in the case of the cedar that clings alone to its rocky cliff, there will be incorporated into that character a strength, a hardiness, a toughness, and a rugged vitality matched only by its beauty and attractiveness that sets it apart from its fellows. Outwardly a Christian's life may appear the worse for wear and tear. Even our Master was a man of sorrows and acquainted with grief. But oh, what a figure set apart he was—sinners were drawn to him and children loved him.

The growth of such character is possible only under adversity. It is something that can be produced only under the inexorable stress and strain of stormy weather. The tree which responds vigorously to the wrenching winds and bending snow grows tough and strong and durable. Inwardly there is the continuous, quiet, unspectacular growth in godliness. The inner life becomes rich, lustrous, and mellow. Built into the very fiber and grain of the soul are a charm and beauty that only blustery weather could possibly produce.

Most of us want to avoid the hard things, the adverse winds, the testing times. Let us not. They are God's method of making special timber for adorning his sanctuary.

The individual whose life has been exposed to stormy weather and survived the strain is most often the one with a quiet inner calm, a sweet serenity of spirit.

Beyond and above this, the picturesque trees above timberline—the battered, beaten, bent, and beautiful trees of the high country—possess the finest aroma. Their wood is impregnated with pitch and resins that act as lubricants between the flexing fibers of their wind-tossed timber. When this wood is sawn and planed and shaped under the master craftsman's cutting tools, its fragrance fills the air and all the building.

Such perfume is produced only by adversity.

God give me grace to thank you for hardship.

When I do, my life and spirit will grow beautifully winsome—not bitter or cynical.

Fire

Open your doors, O Lebanon, that the fire may devour your cedars! Wail, O fir tree and cypress, for the cedar has fallen; because the glorious and lofty trees are laid waste! Wail, O you oaks of Bashan, for the thick and inaccessible forest [on the steep mountain side] has in flames been felled—Zec 11:1-2, Amplified Bible

THE ONCE MAGNIFICENT FORESTS of Lebanon are today but a tiny fragment, a sad remnant of their former splendor. It is true man's wasteful and indiscriminate cutting accounts for much of the loss. Solomon alone sent 183,300 hewers, fellers, and workers into those fine forests. But the other cause of their decline has been from burning. Some of the forest fires were started through carelessness of shepherds, settlers, or woodcutters. Others were ignited by natural causes like lightning.

The growth of forest trees all over the world is closely linked with fire. Fire is a determining factor in the survival of certain species. For instance some trees are fire-resistant. Their thick, tough, corklike bark will scarcely burn at all, so that they can withstand hot fires that would destroy other species. The oaks of dry regions are typical of this fire-resistant type, so are the Douglas firs of our Pacific region. This does not mean that they will not burn at all; it simply implies that they can endure and survive where their fellows sometimes succumb.

One of the species most sensitive to fire are the cedars. Not only do they burn readily and intensely but, once fire has swept through their stand, they are often supplanted by other trees. Or if other species are not growing adjacent to them, their stand may be replaced by inferior forms of brush and undergrowth. Though cedars grow in moist, well-watered regions, they are, nevertheless, extremely susceptible to fire damage and are readily fire-killed.

In many forests, fires burn more fiercely and with greater devastation because brush and brambles and undergrowth become established around the trees. A very clear picture of this is given in Judges 9:15: "And the bramble said unto the trees, if in truth ye anoint me king over you, then come and put your trust in my shadow: and if not, let fire come out of the bramble, and devour the cedars of Lebanon."

Lightning also frequently strikes trees that stand out in exposed sites on ridges or open country. If a tree has dead or dry wood it may be set ablaze. Green, vigorous, luxuriant trees are not so apt to burn, though they may be scarred or split or shattered by the electrical discharge that goes to ground.

The likelihood of such a calamity befalling a strong, green vigorously growing tree is much less than for one which is dried up, diseased, or cumbered with dead wood. The rich, dense foliage of a healthy cedar, moreover, so shades the soil beneath it that it precludes brush and brambles from encircling it. So the chances of its being burned are more remote.

In the Word of God, fire, especially as it is used in the Old Testament, represents the great judgments of God in administering justice to mortal man. Fire especially applies to his own children, those who are his chosen ones, those who have known him but who have gone astray.

As Christians we are inclined to forget that our Heavenly Father who is all love and mercy and compassion to us is at the same time altogether righteous, holy, just, and severe in disciplining those who disobey.

In a very real sense one of the most serious difficulties an earnest Christian faces in his conduct on earth is found in the area of his intimate contact with non-Christians.

In this realm lies the ever present temptation to become too closely involved with the life, enterprise, and interests of the world. Many of these associations may appear perfectly legitimate and even worthwhile, but they may not necessarily be of merit in God's mind. Like the brambles and underbrush entwining themselves around the trunks of the cedars, they slowly but inexorably enmesh us in an apparently harmless though potentially flammable association.

The Christian who is keen for God and growing in Christ should not allow the entanglements of the world to wrap themselves around him. This is precisely what happened to "righteous Lot," who, when fire fell on Sodom and Gomorrah, was stripped of everything and came within a hairsbreadth of losing his own life. It was only the angels' direct intervention and Abraham's prayers for his survival that saved him from disaster.

When we become too closely identified with

the world in which we live, disaster may stalk us and even engulf us in its rushing fury, just the way fire sweeps through the underbrush to set the cedars alight.

God makes it very clear that judgment must first begin with his own people (1 Pe 4:17-18). And we must consistently remind ourselves that though he is longsuffering, and patient in his dealing with us, there are times when a Christian who compromises with the world will be punished promptly and with awesome severity. On occasion, like a bolt of lightning flashing from a thundercloud, death may even descend to consume the living tree. This is what happened to Ananias and Sapphira, who dropped dead when they tried to deceive God over a real estate transaction (Acts 5:1-11).

Jesus entreated his Father that though we are in the world, we would not be of it (Jn 17:14-17). We can do no better than pray the same prayer ourselves. Moreover, God expects us to use the discretion he has given us to detect dangerous situations when they present themsleves. He expects us to have the simple courage to refuse unnecessary entanglements.

This is best assured when we are growing steadily in him.

Because the cedars are relatively thin-barked trees, readily susceptible to fire, they are a valid example of the Christian life. In my growth in

God there needs to be a keen sensitivity to the reproof and correction of the Spirit. Otherwise, judgment, when it comes, will prove to be a burning experience. It will leave an indelible scar, like those on a charred tree, on my careless character.

"For our God is [indeed] a consuming fire" (Heb 12:29).

Space

I will bring healing to their crushed spirits; in free mercy I will give them back my love; my vengeance has passed them by. I will be morning dew, to make Israel grow as the lilies grow, strike roots deep as the forest of Lebanon. Those branches shall spread, it shall become fair as the olive, fragrant as Lebanon cedar.
—Hos 14:4-6, Knox translation

IN SCIENTIFIC TERMINOLOGY there is a law which states that nature will not tolerate a vacuum. This applies equally whether the vacuum be created by artificial, mechanical means within a laboratory retort, or whether it be in a biological sense in the natural realm.

For example, when a forest fire has swept through a stand of timber, leaving in its wake a bare burn that is bereft of life, a biological blank or vacuum has been created. Or if during a gusting gale trees are uprooted and crash to the earth leaving great gaps in the forest canopy, a biological vacuum has been established.

Nature will not tolerate such a situation. At once biological processes are set in motion to restore some sort of life and growth to the barren spot. It may commence with only lowly mosses, lichens, and annuals. Subsequently grass and pioneer plants such as poplar, willow, and other short-lived trees will invade the space. These are but forerunners of the climax vegetation of tall, long-lived trees that will eventually supplant the pioneers to produce a permanent forest.

This is but a bird's-eye view of the continuous contest which proceeds in the plant kingdom for space, for room to grow, for a place to spread in splendor.

Trees that grow together too tightly in dense groves will actually smother and stunt each other. If in the fierce competition to find space for their spreading limbs and roots some succumb, the vacancy left by their death is promptly occupied by the surviving trees around. This immediate response to space is one of the most powerful impulses that control and determine the degree of growth in a virile tree.

A vigorous cedar of Lebanon, its head towering well over one hundred feet into the sun, its massive, widespread horizontal limbs far outstretched for air and dew and mist, its roots reaching far in search of water and nutrients from the soil, requires a tremendous amount of space in order to thrive. This is especially true of individual trees which often produce a number of trunks from the same base, spreading themselves splendidly in a display of green glory.

There were no other trees in all of Palestine to compare with the magnificent cedars of Lebanon. To those who saw them they were a thrilling sight as they grew to such grandeur on their rock-ribbed mountains. And one of the most important reasons why they attained such stature was that they had space—ample, open room—in which to flourish.

Coming now to the Christian life, it is interesting to observe the same law of response to space at work in human hearts.

Jesus himself made reference to it in his parable about the sower and the seed. He emphasized how, in the growth of some plants, they were actually choked out by the competition from others (see Mt 13:7, 22). There was simply a lack of sufficient space in which to survive.

In the Christian life, as in the life of a tree, we must face the fact that we are continually crowded and surrounded by earthly attractions, by human philosophies, by people with worldly concepts.

Now God has very definite, though at times drastic, measures for eliminating some of this competition from our lives. He literally clears away the encroaching trees and undergrowth by his fires of discipline or storms of suffering and sorrow.

If a loved one or a friend or a business associate begins to gradually dominate my life and cramp my Christian growth, God may see fit to remove him or her. The sudden gap left in my life may seem an appalling loss, but he did it in love to make more room for me to grow in himself. He wants me to respond with new affection and fresh devotion to Christ.

Perhaps my profession, my career, my business, has become the overshadowing thing in my life. It is stifling my growth in God. It dominates my desires. I find myself becoming indifferent to Christ's claims. A falling off in correspondence with God becomes apparent in my conduct.

God in mighty mercy and jealous love for his child may bring my career tumbling down around me. My business may be blown away in the winds of adversity. Then suddenly there is space and time and opportunity for me to spread myself before him in repentance. Only there will I sense the depth of his concern for me. Our beautiful head passage from Hosea puts it so clearly: crushed spirits will be healed, love will be restored, and the still dews of his quietness will be upon my outstretched limbs. Again, the very roots of my being will lay hold afresh on Christ, they will draw their strength from God. Out of it all, my life will exude the fragrance of a revitalized and vigorous growth.

It should be emphasized that everything depends upon how I respond to this outer stimulus of space that God clears around me.

I can recoil from the apparent disaster of his discipline, growing bitter, scarred, and cynical. Or I can reach out to grasp God, spreading myself penitently in his presence to grow stronger than ever: this because I realize it is he who has done it in love.

Some of the finest and most noble cedars stand all alone, set apart among their crowded fellows. The man or woman who grows mighty in God discovers, too, that he must be set apart from the clamorous commotion of the common crowd.

Minerals

As therefore you have received the Christ, even Jesus our Lord, live and act in vital union with Him; having the roots of your being firmly planted in Him, and continually building yourselves up in Him, and always being increasingly confirmed in the faith as you were taught it, abounding in it with thanksgiving.
—Col 2:6-7, Weymouth translation

AT THE BEGINNING of this series of studies it was stated that a tree *does not grow itself.* Rather it grows in response to certain stimuli or specific conditions which surround it.

Now that portion of a tree which we refer to as the root system that is below the surface of the ground is surrounded by soil. Reduced to very simple terms we may say that soil consists of inorganic matter and organic matter. Or in layman's language we call them minerals and humus.

Minerals in the soil are derived from the weathering of rock. They have their origin either in the bedrock upon which the soil rests, or they have been transported from afar and distributed across the land by glaciation, flooding, wind erosion, or other physical forces of weathering.

It is perfectly proper to say, therefore, that rock in the form of minerals comprises a most important part of the tree's total environment. It is, moreover, common knowledge that the vigor and quality and strength of any vegetation are determined in large measure by the mineral content of the soil upon which it is growing. A tree rooted in rich soil produces rich foliage and strong growth. One struggling on sickly, thin, leached-out land will be correspondingly weak and stunted.

It is no accident or mere chance that the cedars of Lebanon are trees of tremendous size and strength. Their natural habitat is the mineral-rich mountains of Syria. Those high rock ridges are ideal for timber.

The tireless roots of the forest giants penetrated and honey-combed the soil that lay upon those mountains, drawing from it minerals which would be built up into the very tissues and fibers of the timber. It was not just happenstance that these cedars have towering trunks that stand like tall spires upon the mountainside. Their roots are bound up with the very soil upon which they grow.

What a sublime picture this is of the Christian whose life is now rooted and grounded in Christ Jesus!

Again and again throughout Scripture the inspired writers have used the metaphor of our God as a rock. For example: "I will publish the name of the Lord: ascribe ye greatness unto our God. He is the Rock, his work is perfect" (Dt 32:2-4).

In the spiritual realm the strength and stamina of my character will depend upon the sort of material from which it is built. It will be conditioned by the source from which I draw spiritual sustenance. The decision as to where I choose to sink my spiritual roots and on what I prefer to feed my mind and heart and soul rests with me.

Christ Jesus offers himself as a sure rock upon which a man can establish his character. In the verse at the head of this study I am told clearly and concisely that the very roots of my being have been *planted in him* just as God chose to plant the cedars in the high hills of Lebanon.

Having been established in such a setting with all the resources of Christ made available to me, there is no reason why I shouldn't grow except for my own indolence, my reluctance to put out an effort to search for the riches in him just as the tree roots search the soil.

One of the interesting things about the root system of a tree is that very often it actually exceeds in size and scale the total mass of the trunk, limbs, and leaves which can be seen above the ground. It is not unusual for a tree to have miles of roots and rootlets.

The great tasks of this underground network are not only to anchor the tree to the ground but—much more important—to search out and absorb the available nutrients in the soil. By a very complex process the minerals are absorbed through the root hairs at the tips of the rootlets which are always growing rapidly. This material is then taken up into the tree and built into the very fibers and tissues of the trunk and branches. This is what gives strength and sturdiness to the entire tree. Yet it must be remembered that all this goes on below ground in silence and without fanfare.

Similarly, if we would grow up into Christ, if we would be built up in him, there must be a quiet searching of his Word; there must be an assimilation of the riches available to us in secret, diligent study.

From cover to cover the Bible is a bold declaration of the precious provisions made for man by his Heavenly Father. It is a revelation of all our resources in Christ. It is rich with promises and truths and eternal principles upon which I can draw for strength of character and stamina of conduct. These are my legitimate heritage. It is up to me to take them, to claim them for myself just as a tree absorbs the minerals from the soil in which it grows.

As I assimilate God's Word it becomes incorporated into the very fiber of my makeup. It becomes life and strength to me. The decision for me is a very simple one. Will I or will I not study the Scriptures? They contain the riches which are mine in Christ Jesus.

If I commit whole chapters to memory, making them mine, I will soon discover God's gracious Spirit doing the building up of my character with the material that I have taken into my mind and heart. Thus I grow from strength to strength.

Rather than learning random verses it is well to master whole *blocks* of the Bible. This gives continuity and coherence to the material in mind. Here are twenty-four passages which if mastered—one each month for only two years—will provide material that can completely transform the fabric of a Christian's life. One cannot absorb these and not grow!

Ex 20:1-21	Mal 3	Rom 8
1 Sa 2:1-10	Mt 5	1 Cor 13
Ps 1	Mt 6	Gal 5
Ps 23	Mt 7	Eph 6
Ps 51	Jn 3	Col 1
Prov 20	Jn 14	Phil 3
Isa 40	Jn 15	Heb 12
Isa 53	Jn 16	Rev 21

Another suggestion for uncovering treasures from the Bible is to read a passage daily in at least two different translations (the more the better). Each reading comes then as a new rendering that reveals the truth and riches not previously discovered.

Finally there is the thrill of what I sometimes call "taking an energetic hike in Scripture"—reading an entire book rapidly at a single sitting to sense its surging story and message for my heart. This will disclose delights and precious new truths of great worth.

Humus

For if we have been planted together in the likeness of his death, we shall be also in the likeness of his resurrection—Rom 6:5

THE PRECEDING STUDY stated that soil is composed of organic and inorganic compounds, that is to say, of humus and minerals. Humus, to put it very simply, is dead or decaying vegetable matter. It is derived from the broken-down cellular structure of plants and trees. Humus is composed of the leaves, twigs, buds, bark, wood, roots, and fruit that have fallen back to the earth to be incorporated into the soil through the processes of decay.

Humus is as important for healthy soils and vegetation as are the minerals. Soils high in humus grow trees and plants with a "bloom." Their foliage shines and glistens with a rich sheen that sets them apart from those grown on poor land.

Humus represents the critical link in the so-called energy conversion cycle which is made up of birth, growth, death, decay, and rebirth. All of life is dependent upon this complex process. It explains why we say there can be no life or growth without there first being death. In fact, the entire biota (living world) is conditioned by death. Life can only come from preexisting life which is made available through death. For example, in a forest a tree takes root, runs its life course, comes to the end of its growth, then one day under a fierce storm crashes back to the earth. Immediately the agents of decay go to work on the mass of splintered wood, reducing it to humus. Soon other tree seedlings take root in the decomposing material and a new array of life emerges from the dead form. Through the death of one, new life has been imparted to many others.

It is startling to discover this same principle running throughout the Bible. From beginning to end we find the theme that spiritual life is

dependent upon sacrificial death. The supreme
and universal application of this principle came at
Calvary. God himself saw that it was imperative
he himself should die in the form of his own Son
in order that there might be made available to all
men of all time the opportunity for them to be
born anew into his life, or as the head verse puts
it, "planted together in the likeness of his death."
This then enables us to grow up into the life of his
resurrection. For it is on the very life of Christ
that we draw our sustenance, exactly as the young
cedar derives new life from the prostrate form of
its predecessor.

This is all a great mystery, but nevertheless a
fact. It is one of the thrilling realities we accept
and act on by simple faith. For just as new
seedlings strike root and grow luxuriantly upon
the fallen trunk of a former forest monarch, so
there is life and growth available to me through
the sacrificial death of the Lord of Glory. Young
Christians are sometimes bewildered by this
principle, yet we are told plainly, "Since by man
came death, by man came also the resurrection of
the dead. For as in Adam all die, even so in Christ
shall all be made alive" (1 Cor 15:21-22).

Now there is a second aspect to the part played
by death in the growth of any living organism.
Actually from the time of birth or even germination every living thing is dying. If we stand long
enough under one of the giant cedars we will

notice a continual dropping of cast-off limbs, twigs, bark, needles, and ripened cones. This material falls in a steady rain beneath the tree adding to the humus of the soil in which it is growing. Not only does it contribute to its own good but also that of all the lesser trees and shrubs growing about its base. Still another benefit is that this removes what would otherwise become diseased.

This daily dying, though it might appear a painful process to the tree, is one of its most wholesome growth activities. Likewise in my daily spiritual life I have to discover that there are areas of my character which can be improved only by severe pruning, either through outright death or by God's cutting hand.

As Jesus put it to his disciples, "Let ... [a man] deny himself [die to his own desires], and take up his cross [that will cut him from his claim to himself], and follow me" (Mk 8:34).

How do I do this in actual practice?

First, I simply recognize the fact that as a Christian there are some desires of the old life to which I must die. Most of these are selfish and self-centered attractions. Paul tells us to reckon ourselves dead to them.

For instance, my natural inclination may be to love exaggerating and telling tall stories. All that this achieves is the inflation of my ego. As a Christian I have to take the position that this tendency simply does not have a place in my conduct. I positively reject it. I count (reckon) myself estranged from it, as having no place for it in me. Immediately at that point it drops off like a falling leaf or dead branch and I become more Christlike on that characteristic.

But many of us are not resolute enough nor earnest enough in our dealings with God to live this way. Then for our own good he steps in and prunes us in what sometimes can be a painful process.

Often after a terrible storm one can walk under the trees and see a veritable carpet of limbs, leaves, twigs, and other debris lying beneath the trees.

How does this work in my spiritual life?

Assume that I continue to indulge my appetite for telling tall stories. One day I may discover that someone has caught me in an outright lie and the upshot is that I am terribly humiliated and mortified. I am in a very real sense broken up over the matter. Now I can do one of two things. Either I can deny it, resent it, protest my innocence, and pretend it was not intended; or I can humble myself, apologize, confess my wrong, and reach out to take this mortification willingly. If I do this the cross has been applied and in dying to myself on this point I have grown into Christ's likeness.

This very simply is the meaning of dying daily.

It may not always be that I am in the wrong. Sometimes it happens that I am accused without a cause. Still it is right for me to accept this cross with gladness. My Lord did when there was no fault found in him. To do this is to be made one with him, to be identified with him, to grow in *him*. Thus from death come resurrection life and newness of character.

As a Christian progresses along this path, over his life steals that ineffable glow resembling the rich foliage of a tree growing in soil charged with humus. The world has less and less claim on his character, he discovers that the old desires are losing their attraction. He is set free from the world. *He is alive unto God.*

Perils

Therefore as a fire devoureth the stubble, and the flame consumeth the chaff, so their root shall be rottenness, and their blossom shall go up as dust; because they have cast away the law of the Lord of hosts, and despised the word of the Holy One of Israel—Isa 5:24

EVERY LIVING ORGANISM is surrounded by perils of some sort. This is the very pattern and essence of biological behavior on this planet. The whole life and existence, whether of individuals or entire species, is conditioned by danger of death. The instant a man or a tree is born it is set on course to die. It is surrounded on every side by the agencies of death which, for lack of a better, all-inclusive term, I have called "perils." Only so long as the life forces of growth and renewal within the organism exceed the destructive forces of disintegration and death from without will it survive.

It is the principle of preying on and being preyed upon which underlies all existence. As pointed out in the chapter on humus, all life is governed by the energy conversion cycle whereby the continuous cycle of birth, growth, life, death, decay—birth, growth, life, death, decay, and so on, proceeds uninterrupted. The Buddhists, without hope in God, refer to this as "being chained to the wheel of life." A more apt expression would be "chained to the wheel of death."

In the design of natural life it can be clearly seen how any living organism is continually surrounded by perils that potentially spell death. In the case of a tree there are innumerable diseases that may attack the foliage, the trunk, the blossoms, the seed, or the roots. To survive in their own struggle for existence the bacteria or virus that produces the disease must perpetuate itself at the expense of the life of the tree.

The same thing is true of the insect pests which

often attack trees. Bark beetles may be riddling the trunk, or nematodes invading the root system, or moths, aphids, and leafhoppers feeding on the foliage.

Sometimes the peril is more conspicuous than the subtle danger from insects or disease. Storm-broken wood may be invaded by the spores of fungi, mosses, or lichens that begin their deadly work of decay.

Beyond this the peril may be outright physical damage and destruction from animals: seedlings gnawed by rodents; a sapling shredded by a buck polishing the velvet from his antlers for the fall rut; a mature tree damaged by a porcupine feeding on his favorite bark.

All of these, whether moss or mouse, buck or bacteria, are really predators preying upon the tree. Whether or not it survives or succumbs to these outer simuli depends directly upon one thing and one thing only—the health and vitality of its inner life. A strong, sturdy, rapidly growing tree will react swiftly and surely to the attacks made upon it. Disease organisms will not find a footing; spores of decay will be discouraged; damage from animal depredations will be rapidly repaired.

But let it be repeated. All this is possible only if and when the tree itself is in optimum health, when there is surging through it the full force of a vigorous, energetic inner life.

The cedars of Lebanon are unique in possessing properties that make their wood resistant to insects, virtually impervious to decay, and extremely durable. This is why they are capable of growing into fine fragrant timber suitable for the temple.

In the economy of God, he saw clearly that because death dominated the earth, the only way its power and domination could be broken was for himself, in Christ, to enter directly into the cycle of birth, growth, life, and death upon our planet. Christ Jesus was born of a virgin, grew up among men, lived and moved among us, then died for us. But, marvel of marvels, his body did not decay (Ps 16:10). Instead of being chained to the cycle, he shattered its power and rose directly from the dead. No wonder Christians shout, "Death is swallowed up in victory. O death, where is thy sting? O grave, where is thy victory?" (1 Cor 15:54-55).

What a triumph!

The shackles that had chained men to the wheel of death on this planet have been snapped.

This is the magnificent overcoming life made available to man through the resurrection of Christ.

This inner life must surge through me in full flowing strength if I am to triumph over the attacks of evil all around me.

The Christian life is a perilous life; it is

threatened with danger and destruction on every hand.

> We are troubled on every side, yet not distressed; we are perplexed, but not in despair; persecuted, but not forsaken; cast down, but not destroyed; always bearing about in the body the dying of the Lord Jesus, that the life [resurrection] also of Jesus might be made manifest in our body (2 Cor 4:8-10).

This is the exact picture of how a virile Christian responds to the stimuli of perils which encircle him.

How do I realize this resurrection life within?

How do I acquire this vitality to counteract all the forces of evil and sin and despair that surround me in a dying and despairing world?

By calmly claiming and acting on God's own declaration: "Ye are of God, little children, and have overcome them: because greater is he [Christ] that is in you, than he [Satan] that is in the world" (1 Jn 4:4).

This takes trust, simple faith, implicit confidence in God. Faith is more than mere belief; it is an absolute conviction, an implicit confidence that gives me the grit *to act on* and *respond to* the declarations of divine truth.

Now if I want my faith in God to grow, the way to stimulate it vigorously is to remind myself always of his absolute faithfulness and utter reliability to me, his child.

God cannot betray either himself or his children.

As I act on this realization, he unfailingly imparts to me, by the Spirit, his own abounding resurrection life of growth in godliness that counteracts every peril and perplexity. I know of a surety that *he is alive* and because he is alive I, too, shall live.

It is when I lose confidence in God's Word to me that I leave myself wide open to an invasion of doubt and sin and despair that can only result in rottenness and weakness within (see head verse).

"This is the victory that hath overcome the world, even our faith" (1 Jn 5:4, A.S.V.).

Darkness

*And if thou draw out thy soul to the hungry,
and satify the afflicted soul; then shall thy light
rise in obscurity, and thy darkness be as the noon
day: and the Lord shall guide thee continually,
and satisfy thy soul in drought, and make fat
thy bones: and thou shalt be like a watered
garden, and like a spring of water, whose waters
fail not*—Isa 58:10-11

BECAUSE OF THE PHYSICAL LAWS which control the
rotation of the earth upon its own axis, it is a

natural phenomenon that there should be both light and darkness upon the planet.

Depending upon the season of the year and the geographical location of any given tree, it will be exposed to light for a portion of each twenty-four hour period and plunged into darkness for the balance of the time. This is one of the straight-forward facts that make night, or darkness, one of the stimuli that condition its growth.

During darkness, photosynthesis, which can only proceed under the impulse of light, ceases. Respiration, however, goes on. Respiration is the process whereby carbohydrates, especially dextrose, formed by photosynthesis, are oxidized (burned slowly) within the tree to energize all its vital life functions. This process takes oxygen out of the air and combines it with dextrose to produce energy, giving off ordinary water and carbon dioxide as by-products.

In other words, the tree's response to darkness is active life. During darkness ample energy is generated to fulfill the essential functions of life processes within the tree.

Darkness also normally provides respite from excessive heat. It evens out and moderates temperatures within a tree so that photosynthesis can proceed at an optimum rate when sunlight is available, assuring maximum growth. High internal temperatures (exceeding 120 degrees) can be very damaging to even the sturdiest tree.

Darkness brings dew and refreshment to the foliage of the tree. In mountainous country like Lebanon, where the forests lie close to the sea, nighttime brings its banks of cloud and mist and fog that enshroud the trees in refreshing coolness, saturating the cedars with mineral-laden moisture from the ocean deeps.

In short, darkness is the time during which a tree restores its strength, replenishes its energy, refreshes its fevered life, and finds respite from the heat and activity of the day.

Among Christians there is a decided aversion to darkness. Probably this is because in the Bible darkness is so often associated with evil. Because of this we draw back from the very thought of darkness as if it could contain nothing but ill.

In a spiritual sense we must discover the meaning of darkness in two dimensions, especially as it relates to the formation of Christian character. First there is the darkness of unbelief all around us: the darkness of a world separated from God who is the source of all light; the darkness of men and women who grope for that light, but who have not met the Man of Galilee in the light of his own glorious life and compassion for them.

How am I to respond to such darkness around me? Will I recoil from it? Will I withdraw from those unfortunate ones who walk in such darkness? Or will I go out into it eagerly seeking to lead some of them to my Master? If I do, the outcome will startle me. Even that darkness will be transformed into light and life and energy when men meet my Master. (Read the head verse carefully).

One of the tremendous personal thrills, known only to a true child of God, is the delight of introducing a soul in darkness to his own Heavenly Father and Christ Jesus his Saviour, the light of the world. Such an experience energizes and vitalizes a Christian's entire life beyond the power of words to describe. It makes his inner life a bright adventure despite the darkness around him.

The second aspect in which a Christian must understand darkness pertains to his own personal life. We are given no guarantee by God that all our days on earth will be nothing but brightness. It is an inexorable law of life, as sure as the rotation of the earth, that for all of us there are going to be some tears and sighs, some sorrow and sadness, some dark periods of disappointment and despair.

Often these are times and events over which we have no control whatever. They come as swiftly and surely as darkness in the desert. How am I going to respond to their apparent oppression? How will I react to these seeming reverses that come to me as stimuli in disguise?

Am I going to rebel against them because they

bring a sudden lull into my feverish activity, because they bog down my busy life, because they curtail my ambitious aspirations?

Or, contrariwise, will I accept them calmly as coming from the hand of my Heavenly Father for my own well-being? After all, it is perfectly possible to walk in the dark unafraid, undisturbed, and undismayed—"for thou art with me."

Christians at times are so caught up in being busy about many things that God deliberately lets darkness descend around them just so he can have a chance to take a quiet walk with them alone for a change. There in the coolness and stillness, frustrated souls are refreshed, the fever of life is forgotten, and men become "like a watered garden."

In the darkness lies part of the secret to a character that is wholesome, fruitful, radiant, yet balanced in its godly behavior. For some of us it is only in the darkness we dare draw so close to Christ that we later come away with the myrrh and frankincense of his own presence upon us.

It is only in the darkness that I discover something of the sweet fellowship of his suffering—taste a little of the awesome agony he endured for me in the darkness of Gethsemane.

In the darkness I understand at last something of those wondrous words, "not my will, but thine."

Rest

And he shall be like a tree planted by the rivers of water, that bringeth forth his fruit in his season; his leaf also shall not wither; and whatsoever he doeth shall prosper—Ps 1:3

ONE OF THE CONDITIONS most frequently forgotten in thinking about the growth of a tree is rest. Or, to put it in technical terminology, dormancy. In northern climes winter is the period or season of rest. In tropical regions it is generally the hot, dry season of the year when trees and plants find respite from rapid growth.

It is important to understand that dormancy is not death. A tree may appear to be dead, it is true. The leaves of deciduous trees will be all stripped off in the fall leaving a stark skeleton. The tree is nevertheless very much alive—but at rest.

In the case of conifers and evergreens like the cedars of Lebanon the needles are not all shed at once, so that the tree appears to be green and growing at all seasons. Actually this is not so, for during winter these trees, too, are dormant and at rest.

In the design of living things, whether plants or animals, it has been ordained that their bodily structure and strength should be rested and restored periodically. This is conducive to optimum growth. In this connection it is of interest to note that even God himself saw fit to rest after completing his creative enterprises throughout the universe.

Dormancy in a tree occupies a specific season. This season of rest is the one which just precedes the springtime of active and accelerated growth. It is really the time of peaceful preparation for the drastic demands of growth. It is the time of rebuilding wornout cells and reconditioning tired tissues. All of this is in preparation for the upsurge of the vigorous spring.

In a certain sense the period of rest is one of the

most important throughout the entire year. It is the season when a tree becomes fully refitted for the exhausting demands that will be made upon it during the long rigorous growing season when new wood is added to its structure and fresh fruit is borne upon its boughs.

So we may say in all accuracy that in order to grow and flourish in season a tree must also rest and relax out of season.

Precisely the same principle applies in the total spiritual, mental, and emotional life of the Christian. There is an erroneous concept common to many children of God that to be effective they must be always active. There is the idea abroad that one must be always "on the go for God."

Yet even our Lord and Master, Jesus Christ, when he moved among us as the God-Man, found it imperative to withdraw from the activity of his busy life and take time to rest. Again and again we find him slipping away to some quiet spot on a mountainside or across the lake where he could be alone and still for refreshment of body, mind, and spirit. These were interludes of quiet communion with his Father.

In each of the preceding chapters it has been emphasized that man has his part to play in the decisions which determine his growth in character. *When I deliberately set myself TO DO what God requires of me, responding positively to the stimuli from himself, then he performs his part in seeing to it that* MY LIFE DOES TAKE ON THE CHARACTER OF CHRIST.

This is equally true of rest. It is in the very makeup of life that we are bound to encounter times when we have gotten beyond our strength and stamina. Then we will hear the Spirit's gentle voice saying, "Come ye yourselves apart . . . , and rest a while" (Mk 6:31).

Again the vital question is, "Will I or won't I respond to this warm invitation?" I can claim to be too busy; that there simply isn't time; that there are too many others depending on me; that I'm tough and can take it; or that I'd rather wear out than rust out.

Each of these may be legitimate and logical replies but they are not necessarily either wise or godly.

Proof of this lies in the number of Christians who collapse under the strain and pressure and tension of twentieth-century society.

Sometimes God, in a mercy which we cannot comprehend, has to deliberately compel us to take an enforced rest for a season. Illness, sudden reverses, or chilling circumstances come like the dark, cold grip of winter upon a Christian, compelling him to cease from his busyness.

Then we hear the plaintive cry, "Why did this have to happen to me?" or "Why am I out in the cold?" "What is the sense of all this suffering?"

"Why can't I keep going for God?"

The answer is a simple one.

I do not honestly believe God is capable of doing his work in the world without my feverish human efforts.

When I reach the place where I have implicit confidence in God's ability to manage not only the affairs of the world but also mine, as I entrust them to him, I will have found the place of rest.

This is borne out very clearly in Hebrews 4:9-10: "There remaineth therefore a rest to the people of God. For he that is entered into his rest, he also hath ceased from his own works [busyness], as God did from his."

It is not always easy to simply step aside into solitude and rest and quietness. But unless I learn how, my entire growth in God will be endangered.

As a simple first step in this direction may I suggest the reader take twenty minutes each day to go out and walk alone—a brisk walk—only smiling to strangers—deliberately looking for the beauty and handiwork of God in the natural world about him, and inwardly adoring the Lord for who he is. Leave the worries and work at home or in the office. It will prove to be a tonic, a rest that results in growth in God.

Most of us have never learned the humble though powerful practice of concentrating on Christ. Outside, walking alone, away from the usual surroundings which remind us of our feverish workaday world, we can give our hearts a chance to center their interest and affection on him.

It is a simple, humble habit. Perhaps it is too ordinary for most men.

But to walk with God means just that—daily.

This in essence is the secret of rest. It is the time of waiting, of communing with God the Father, of coming to Christ, of being inwardly conscious of the Holy Spirit's gentle voice entreating me to lift up my soul to him who, when he was among us, said, "Come unto me, all ye that labour and are heavy laden, and I will give you rest" (Mt 11:28).

And having come, I will be refreshed and fitted for new growth in God during future days.